ONE
BIG
TIME

WAVE BOOKS

ONE BIG TIME

LISA
FISH
MAN

SEATTLE / NEW YORK

Published by Wave Books
www.wavepoetry.com
Copyright © 2025 by Lisa Fishman
All rights reserved
Wave Books titles are distributed to the trade by
Consortium Book Sales and Distribution
Phone: 800-283-3572 / SAN 631-760X
Library of Congress Cataloging-in-Publication Data
Names: Fishman, Lisa, 1966– author.
Title: One big time / Lisa Fishman.
Description: First edition. | Seattle : Wave Books, 2025.
Identifiers: LCCN 2024038732 | ISBN 9798891060142 (paperback)
Subjects: LCGFT: Poetry.
Classification: LCC PS3556.I814572 O54 2025
DDC 811/.54—dc23/eng/20240910
LC record available at https://lccn.loc.gov/2024038732
Designed by Crisis
Printed in the United States of America
9 8 7 6 5 4 3 2 1
First Edition
Wave Books 123

TABLE OF DAYS, 2020

July 10-13 —— 3

July 14 —— 15

July 15 —— 21

July 16-18 —— 27

July 19 —— 33

July 20 —— 39

July 21-22 —— 43

July 23-24 —— 49

JULY
10-13

    you could just say
       not anything
      in the forest
under hemlock

      waterbeing going by

    meant to write waterbody

but it came out waterbeing
under treebody

———

it's different outside how the ground is
warm: springy, moss-covered and
root-traversed, very warm
            underfoot, under trees'
   shade

     the borrowed cabin's
new laminate floor makes your feet
very cold

   what else
  for the loves

———

    The current of the lake is swift
    like a river
    is it a river? I ask but no one
    says yes or no one
    knows
    because it is a lake
    that merges w/other lakes
    I ask for a map but
               none appears

    Water being
    one that flows: F L O W - e r
                   gets to
        open in
        the swim
    morning, night &
      in between
   all day
        Day all a bird
     sound makes
  off to the side
          —can't say which direction but you know
  over the shoulder, not far

  the names of friends pop in
  across the page and then
  my father's handwriting for a
  few words where I see
  he made his *f*'s and *g*'s
  different from mine

    there's the water

moving swiftly

    this forest

———

Have not found the passage to the other lake
just to the left of downed trees   where someone pointed
I set off
in my boat twice and the
first time did not find it &
                the second time
    did not find it

In between he asked
            if I found it
No I said but will look again
It's marshy he said
      and I set off again
looking more closely
where you might get thru
a marshy, hidden passage
but it stayed hidden
so I'll look again
although I'd really like to go in the other direction
with the current, which is consistent
every day—it blows or moves
              from north to south

ask why
when he brings a map

Also looked for the passage on foot
(banked the boat on "Crown land")
across the water
but only found myself lost,
or rather, surprised
ea. time I came out of the
        forest to the water
to see where I was
    on the shoreline
& it seemed I kept ending up in
    the same place
even tho that makes no sense at all

actually it seemed I <u>was</u> in a different place
but that a landmark I'd noted somewhere else
had shifted too and was now in the different place
where <u>I</u> was, which I understand
is impossible

PS: Evergreens were dying all the way up the U. P.
                                            but not here

Two weeks is better than one week
which reminds me
this is quarantine, by law
staying in place
14 days
Border Control will call every day
they said, but haven't yet

I make a list:
two moose one loon the single
constant chipmunk
multiple birds
no boats except a metal row

& scruffy kayak

cloud   sky

temptation

to plainest words

Folded over, toward the sun
                 to warm up
stretched out
  upside down
where the sky is
  water

      Then I love the hemlock I am sitting under
          on the mossbed, not afraid
          to lean against it how one sits
          against a tree but usually
          I don't because of dog pee
             in the park

          He is giant, the hemlock
             is a he
             today

———

Don't go type but fix something
already here
or the dishes
need washing
and you shd brush yr hair
once in a while

write Amy

———

    All the different kinds of moss have names

        but of course they really don't

DAWN TO DUSK

Dear
Anyone
With or Without
Names

        To
        Open

                Day-and-night
                Unselving with
                Shushing wind at however many
                Knots

They do come through you
and set you down

Kyger said: seed syllables

———

you don't see faces in the milkweed
only monarchs, the opposite
of kings

Must make time
[to]
    SWIM : S - W - I - M

    Sleek widening instant's magnet

TIME : T - I - M - E

    Tremor
    Is
    Many
    Elders

    Tree
    Is
    Many
    Elders

Try
ing
mouth's
enterior
    at the foot of a hemlock
        over roots

and down there is the lake
full of fish
and there is no reason
to stop writing

so you stay
in the sun
with the trees
a bit longer
all day

keeping away the people
who think I took their bucket,
a yellow minnow bucket
full of minnows—
I did not.
But no one else is here and so
it's unexplained.

No other people, I mean.
There are many
others, creatures.
One of them must have wanted minnows
and the yellow bucket too.

JULY
14

5:30 a.m.
Morning star and Crescent moon
in dusky light (orange red purple)
an hour later, light's bright yellow
then silvery yellow
then clear or no color, transparent
light

A novel confused me just this year
bc she was talking about dusk
first thing in the morning, at dawn
so I looked into it and sure enough
dusk is really
a quality of light, not a time of day
(light with colors)

& yesterday "at dusk"
the dusky light was blue

I notice not being tempted
      to say so what

———

Where the lake cuts through the forest it does not show you.

Go around.

Where a bird or human ate a fish
clean on the rock, you can see
a fish is all spine
& minimal skull.

Did speak with the government agent,
Lena, who said "that's awesome"
when I answered her question
"I'm here to write" I said
but mostly I've swum (didn't say)

———

Pennefather Township's
not where I am.

Present location
for nine more days:
    up hwy 129
north of Thessalon
        Ontario

North of U. S.
    Undone States

    NORTH

    Nearly
    Out of
    Reach, she
    Talks not to
    Herself

Penniless father
wrote thousands of letters
    riches
like bread and butter

Stones give off heat in the water
so swim near the old ones
if you want to be warm
  under water
is a daughter
unsure about the
sky

———

I think a bird could have taken
the missing yellow minnow bucket
bc a gull flew down & grabbed
a fish out of the lake right beside me
then flew in a circle around me, wondering?
just before dusk

JULY 15

Find the trees
liking rain, raising a ruckus
   on the fifth day
everything silver
in a big rain
   water & sky can't tell
the difference between themselves

   BLUR

   Be-
   Longing
   Unto
   Rain

the "Crown land" disappears
what a sound
and as soon
as you can write it down
it stops
& things are there again
water, sky, forest across
the lake
and these
8 trees right here
no, 10—that's the number
from the window
for the rain
still's falling, less so

Blame the rain
for the rhyme
in your ear

———

Water lilies not to be told
but a loon comes around

        I dropped this pencil
    in the lake
           and it floated, to my surprise

but it's wood
    of course it floated
to my surprise

so steal the boat
for a night or two, that transgression
               self sets out

———

Not really knowing
what day it is, utopian
swimming in a light rain
7-15-20

2 parts of land are connected by a footbridge
of logs falling down
from the '30s? over a narrow
                channel

on this side the water's called something

on that side the water's called something else

All five lakes are connected here
or, one big waterbody has
                    5 names

Tried to go thru
the channel today as usual
but not enough water even though
it was raining

+ some water lilies that were white
                the other days
are pink today, not open yet
it seems they turn pink in the rain

Eternity is in love, Wm Blake?

———

How slowly a bear
eats a salmon
holding the fish
in its hands/paws/claws
Did not see this in person
but watched a video to see
if that spine on the rock yesterday
meant a bear had eaten that fish
but no: bears eat all the bones
the spine and skull

at the same time
as fins and flesh
while the half-body of the fish being held
flops around in the bear's paw (tries to thrash)
& from the open half
of the fish's body, bright red blood
spurts out

———

A loon went under
and came up nowhere
    to be seen
Ghost loon
no ship
yes the day's
unfinished

JULY
16-18

He the neighbor brings a map
with the portage marked:
portage he says, with a French
accent, where I've looked four times
for a PASSAGE
because when he says porTAGE
I hear in my mind, PASSage
when really there is no passage
to go through in a boat—
only a path through the woods
where you can carry your boat (portage)
but I don't know this yet
so I say I'll look again, as if having a map
can change what happens

The five lakes are called:

>   Wakomata, furthest east
>   Jobammageeshig (largest)
>   Huston, west and north, barely connecting to
>   Blue Heaven Lake, but this makes six
>   including Chub
>   & Little Chub

The name of the big one, Jobammageeshig, is said very fast
            so only the first syllable's clear to the visiting ear
& who it was taken from
the map does not show

———

27

A riven
land
a river makes
for now this is
a river valley:
Mississagi
riven
from Ojibwe: *misi-zagi*
"river with a wide mouth"
or from Anishinaabe: *Misi-zaagiing*
"[Those at the] Great River-mouth"
Another account says that in Ojibwe
it's *Misswezahging*: "river with many outlets"

In 1840 a treaty
used the term *leagues* instead of *miles*:
deceit
therefore the Court is hearing
whether Thessalon &
Big Basswood Lake
are rightfully Ojibwe still

———

day 8
beavers are making another lake
across the highway
across a meadow
mown to grass
& metal rowboats from the 1940s
are lined up neatly upside down
once brightly painted green blue red
rusty peeling now

found a Crown sign made of tin
nailed to a post near the beaver pond
Plate #
1024389

———

If the surface is clear
from shore at dawn
you can see straight thru to layered rock
      it's brighter underneath
& a fish just now
      came toward me, then 3 more—
        fish are the ones
I won't eat again
their life's too good
although they do seem to be looking for something
first thing in the morning

JULY 19

Ninth day
the first day
was Saturday
Today's again
Saturday   cooler
    less sunny
I'd like to cut my hair
w/borrowed scissors

———

Here on a rock I see the loon
does not perceive me
as a threat. She ate her lunch
looning around
in circles, going under
& coming back, always within
12 feet of me
but in water if I approach
she goes under
& disappears
       disliking
boat's vibration
in her element

But on the ground a mother grouse
and 2 young freely walk

around the cabin—they're not afraid
of people, said Gillian
that's why they get hunted
but we don't hunt them she said, &
I brought you some eggs
   pullet eggs
and these purple flowers clustered
   on spindly stems—fresh thyme
or is it
oregano

———

Cloud opens
night's mouth
    being written
    in the morning

the sexual words:
ordinary nouns, verbs

now I'm stuck on a rock
in a storm
   being written
   in a boat

under cobwebs
under the claw
of a dead beech
with lush endrunkening cedar fronds
      & other ever
        greens
they breathe you in as you approach

Didn't make it to the high bluffs
where a triangle stone is

storm sent me back
now it's calm but my clothes are wet

everything's wet, anyone said
about something—
the ground? the poem

oh cut the bread

JULY 20

Thunder and rain, no day
today? just 1 room
to be in, two
electric lights   mute them
with towels   nothing's glued
into place

outside,
you can feel yourself thinking
a poem might be possible
as if it's actually wildlife

I used to think it was eros
but no shoes gets you closer
than no clothes

———

Silver light's moving on the water
the birch looks like a poplar
                rain-changed?
        the leaves
are holding still
        and now are not

the lower leaves start moving first
        as if vibration starts low
and there isn't any

       wind, just rain-opened, maybe tingling
                        activating
                  earth

———

The river Niedecker
wrote of minerals
comprising blood
    I think she said we're made of
rock, she of the Rock
           River
but I think she said that
near Lake Superior

———

On the water

    five blue dragonflies

    lightest boat

In the water

    slightly swimming
        in a far-off painting

every detail, one by one

JULY 21–22

the bright red head of the giant
woodpecker who flew so close [i] cd hear
& feel its wings then landed on the hemlock i do
love, and i was only
13 feet away   a few minutes
until it knew, and flew away
has not come back
but the loon is daily (we two
on the water)
and her calls are every evening
from the forest
it seems the rocks are weather
which shapes and moves them
the whole shebang
from everywhere
& outer space

———

tuesday—
did find the por*TAGE* thru the woods!
I carried my boat on the path
into another lake
then crossed into a third part, or another lake
& joined the fish to swim
then sat and lay in the curve or eye of the bluff's
low rock ledge-scape, layers
& shelves down to water

next morning at blue dawn
in the eye-shaped curve of the layered rock
here is matter
fleet, returning
soul as something
else

one may be permitted
to be with it (butterfly on rock wall)
but not go toward—
don't imagine this is anything you know

note that you're writing about the day before

———

Time's named like
      connecting lakes
  —this day, that day—
If you could say water's
continuous, one
      continuous body of water
that goes over land
    here, there,
then of time you cd say
the same: it's one big time
with different names
(yesterday, today, &c)

even so, it's July 22
or was

I looked at the date and waited
to remember what's important about it—
after a second, half a second,
the death date of my dad (2010)

So call your sister, he'd say

———

The forest I carried my boat through
had more paths too
I left the boat in the woods
& walked thru birch trees taller
than possible, much taller
than a white pine i know
to be over 200 yrs old
Can birches live that long
or grow that fast
I ask the guy who lives here
& he says they just grow

JULY 23–24

Evening: another reddish yellow orange stone
escaped being mined in the war
They needed copper, Mike who lives here said,
for the bands around the [   ]
—can't remember what he called them
the copper bands
around artillery shells, those particular
pieces of war

———

Madness of loons last night
(almost wrote *lunes*) chorusing
both to the east of me (lake)
and to the west of me (forest)
Being in the middle of loon calls
helps me name the cardinal directions
then this morning
       (dawn was red)
loons again
       full sun
for the last full day, same as last week
day after day
where'd my vocabulary go

———

Light on the water
(maple) leaves in the light
over water
      from here (under hemlock
above water) i can see
the answer to a question of my mother's:
the "pockmark" pattern on the stones
is the same as the pattern on the water
                          in a light
   current when the lake is quiet
      so
a shift in the medium (element)
repeats the pattern

She's been painting what I'm seeing
although I haven't described it
or sent any photos, haven't
taken any pictures
except yesterday:
      some giant
scarlet mushrooms
on a tree for fungi
photograph well

———

Now a loon's to the north
   sounding excited
   about something

LOON

fill in
words you might see

in the L - O - O - N

    Letters
    One by
    One and
    Now

off you go

(into the boat & head north)

ACKNOWLEDGMENTS

My thanks to poet-editors Billie Chernicoff, David Dodd Lee, Jenny Gropp, Laura Solomon, and Jordan Dunn for publishing longish portions of this book in the following journals, respectively: *SALT II*, *Glacier*, *Oxeye*.